Old North

Old North

Poems

Tony Reevy

Iris Press
Oak Ridge, Tennessee

Copyright © 2013 by Tony Reevy

All rights reserved. No portion of this book may be reproduced in any form or by any means, including electronic storage and retrieval systems, without explicit, prior written permission of the publisher, except for brief passages excerpted for review and critical purposes.

Cover Photo:
Lone Cypress (Columbia, North Carolina)
Copyright © 2013 by Caroline Weaver

Book Design by Robert B. Cumming, Jr.

Library of Congress Cataloging-in-Publication Data

Reevy, Tony.
  [Poems. Selections]
  Old North : poems / Tony Reevy.
      pages cm
  ISBN 978-1-60454-223-3 (paperback : alk. paper) 1. North Carolina—Poetry. I. Title.
  PS3618.E4459O43 2013
  811'.6—dc23
                                         2013012264

Acknowledgments

The author would like to acknowledge the following publications, where many of these poems were first published or are pending first publication:

Bath Avenue Newsletter: "Roan Mountain Pinnacle," "Swan Quarter Landing"
The Blotter Magazine: "Crow Hill"
Caesura: "At Stagville Plantation"
Charlotte Poetry Review: "Uwharrie"
Crab Orchard Review: "Looking for Blind Boy Fuller's Grave," "Revisiting Liberty Warehouse"
Earth and Soul: An Anthology of North Carolina Poetry (Kostroma Writer's Organization, 2001): "In the Sun After a Noon Rain, Woodrow Street"
Lightning in Wartime (Finishing Line Press, 2007): "At a Swimming Pool in the Uwharries," "Before the casino," "Bentonville Battlefield"
Lonzie's Fried Chicken: "Eno Bank"
Magdalena (Pudding House Publications, 2004): "Dinner on the Grounds," "Lyndover Farm"
The Mending Wall: "Brown Mountain"
Natural Bridge: "Buyout"
Out of Line: "The Slave Barn"
Pembroke Magazine: "A Place in All Seasons"
Piedmont Pedlar: "Chicken Catcher's Blues," "Routine Patrol"
The Poet's Page: "Frost Morning"
Sand, Sea, & Sail (Old Mountain Press, 2007): "Summer Dawn, Kitty Hawk"
Silk Road: "Along the State Highway to Franklinville"
South 85: "'Negroes on the main street of Roxboro, North Carolina,'" "Orange Factory Revisited," "Three Portraits"
The Thomas Wolfe Review: "In Riverside Cemetery"
Windhover: "Near Hester, N.C.," "New Legend of the Flat River"
The Writers Network News: "Day's End, Lake Tillery"
Zeus Seduces the Wicked Stepmother in the Saloon of the Gingerbread House (Winterhawk Press, 2008): "Conjure in the Southport Burying Ground," "The Accused"

for Caroline, Lindley and Ian

Contents

Mountains

Roan Mountain Pinnacle 15
Home Village 16
Before the casino 17
Model A Pickup 18
In Riverside Cemetery 19
Brown Mountain 20
The Accused 21
Yadkin Canal 22
Routine Patrol 23

Piedmont

Keeping the faith 27
Dinner on the Grounds 28
Chicken Catcher's Blues 29
The Songwriter Reads About a School Fire 31
Uwharrie 32
Requiem—Pisgah Covered Bridge 34
Dark Mountain 35
At a Swimming Pool in the Uwharries 36
National Forest 37
Day's End, Lake Tillery 38
Along the State Highway to Franklinville 39
Risen 40
"Negroes on the main street of Roxboro, North Carolina" 41
Regulators 42
Crow Hill 43
Farmhouse, White Oak Church Road, Daybreak 44
Near Hester, N.C. 45

Tobacco Town/Tobacco County (Durham, N.C.)

In the Sun After a Noon Rain, Woodrow Street 49
Boulevard Sunrise 50
Durham Street Incident 51
Revisiting Liberty Warehouse 53
Looking for Blind Boy Fuller's Grave 53
North Durham Homeplace 54
The View from the Porch 55
New Legend of the Flat River 56
Roadside Memorial 57
Orange Factory Revisited 58
The Caller Visits the Section Boss 59
Lyndover Farm 60
Along the Old Durham Branch 61
The Slave Barn 62
At Stagville Plantation 63
To the Eno 64
The path dips— 65
Winter Heron 66
Heron Flight 67
Flood Following Drought 68
Two March Sundays 69
Hurricane Wood 70
A Place in All Seasons 71
The Slide 72
Eno Bank 73
At the Little River Trail 74
Little River Bridge 75
Buyout 76

Coast

Warren Plains Depot 79
Bentonville Battlefield 80
New Bypass 81
Three Portraits 82
First Growth Cypress, Williamston, North Carolina 83
When the Fish Come Back 84
Frost Morning 85
At the Old Town Cemetery, Beaufort 86
Boxed Longleafs 87
Conjure in the Southport Burying Ground 88
Summer Dawn, Kitty Hawk 89
Swan Quarter Landing 90

Notes 93

*Fiddlin' Bill Hensley, mountain fiddler,
Asheville, North Carolina*[1]

Mountains

Roan Mountain Pinnacle

Fleshed ferns,
glossed laurel.
Oaks, wind-shaped,
point away
from the blow.

Stunted cedar
like bonsai
entrances.

Green meadow—
trampled grass,
sun-lit, still.

Somehow cool
in July's meridian.

Ghosts sing here
in blue moonlight.
We almost
hear them
now.

Home Village

The mound, Kituwah,
grassy rise crowned
by a fairy circle—
many smokes crowd
close as the Tuckasegee
rushes its edge.
Entry road is rough-
bounded by corn
fields, the river.

All bought back
by coins dropping
in the slots.

The Tuckasegee roars
past Kituwah
to the sea.

Before the Casino

Cherokee was a strip
of neon stores and a
quote museum unquote
selling tomahawks
where Junior put on
a headdress and got
his picture made
with a plains-style
Big Chief.

And the curio-shop cage
with the dancing
chicken—kids asked
for a quarter, dropped
it in the slot, and
the brown-white fowl,
expertly trained, a shock
to onlookers, tried
its wings; then danced,
capered and leapt.

Model A Pickup

The rust-red chassis is
turned turtle a few yards
down the bank. There's
never been a proper road
here, just tracks.

Maybe they took a
joyride up the rails, met
a train. Or did they get
here on a vanished
logging access?

Were they moonshining,
wildcatting firewood,
out for a jaunt?

The truck, only a lump
of twisted steel now,
hides its secrets
in plain view.

In Riverside Cemetery

Wind rushes.

A fish crow,
exiled by mourners,
squawks over
cars roaring to life.

A man stands under solitary cedar,
hands thrust in tweed greatcoat
pockets, long, rambling frame
stooped by age or
effort of saying goodbye.

The great, gangling infant
is lost, o lost, save for a few
papers, books, keys.

The breeze stills. Mist rises
from the French Broad.
Coaches in the switchyard
clang together, part
with blasts of air.

Now, the years of loss
and one's own falling
darkness, like all,
to face alone.

Brown Mountain

The low, dim ridge,
pasty-green in summer heat,
limb-brown and rock-grey
in winter chill, nondescript,
hides its secrets.

Pallid tales—wandering,
star-crossed lovers, Reb
deserters, murdered wives,
hidden stills—
try to explain.

We don't know
what kindles its fires
or, truth be told,
our own.

The Accused[2]

The man didn't kill
for love, maybe, but he
dragged, buried his
sweetheart, swelling with
his child, in the Brushy
Mountain clay. The other
woman stood by, watched.

He did it for love. For
love of a woman, she,
the one with the bloody
knife, standing by.

After the hanging, people
talked on her, said she
witched men, spelled them
to her bed. She grew
ancient as the Brushy
hills, and alone
at the last.

When she died—crack
of thunder, blue
fire, smell of brimstone
in the room.

Yadkin Canal

A whistle echoes
through winter woods;
a freight rumbles
beside the river path.

Past sand, old snags, and
beaver-chewed saplings—
sticking up, sharp,
like Queequeg's teeth.

Around the curve,
a time-smoothed ditch
and a wall of dressed,
unmortared stone.

Leavings of a canal,
dreamed water-road
from far-off mountains
to Salisbury and the sea.

Low sun shines,
silvering the spiked rails,
lighting the wall, black-seamed;
leavened with emerald moss.

What ghost clambers here
at the full moon,
traces jagged stones,
and remembers?

Routine Patrol

I knew his father, Mr. Sims,
he voted for me first
time I ran for sheriff.

Saw him plowing red earth
up there by Sauratown
most every day.

It's a long road
took
that man's son
here
to the Circle K lot.

Lying in a puddle
of blood
mixed up with
glass, oil and spit.

A forty-five in
one hand.

Cash from the till
bulging his pockets.
Mostly ones,
the deputy says.

I got here first,
called out
by the silent alarm.

He ran out
heading for his car.
Saw my car,
wheeled,
raised that forty-five.

Looked a lot like his pa;
it was him or me.

I used my thirty-eight,
put a hole
where his heart
used to be.

*Negroes on the main street
of Roxboro, North Carolina*[3]

Piedmont

Keeping the faith

The old man sits
in half-vacant pews
remembering ladylike
tones of the woman
preacher, bored
inflections of the city
man and—now—coming
back to cheerful
words of new,
young minister. Thinks
away to familiar,
craggy face, church
in the hills, Jonah and
the whale, signs and
portents, fire and
brimstone. Fire and
brimstone.

Dinner on the Grounds

Brush arbor at the
church in Olin, weighty
roof lifted on four-by-
fours. Tables groan
with tomatoes, green-
bean casserole, ham, nine
kinds of pickles. It's
homecoming Sunday,
dinner on the grounds.
The ambulance is gone
with the woman who
gasped and fainted at the
service. They reckon a
heart attack, reckon
she'll be okay. Her pasty
face lingers in my
thoughts flashing from
the rescue squad
truck. The wind stirs
dust under plank tables,
moans like a soft
siren, sways flowers
in the churchyard.

Chicken Catcher's Blues

You gotta be fast
to grab them chickens
Tater Head says,
can't wear no gloves neither
cause it'll slow you down

When you got sixteen thousand
or thereabouts
chickens
in this here chicken house
and six guys to catch em with
You gotta be fast

It's good money, though
and I've done bought
me and my old woman cars
From grabbing them chickens

You can tell the guys
who are gonna last
They don't mind gettin
pecked up or workin
all night

Some of them guys leave
the first time
they see twenty thousand chickens
all in the same place
But, shit, everyone's
gotta have a chicken
to eat. We're just kind
of gettin them started
on the way to the pot

But them birds get
Mad, right mad
when you pick em up
Old Baby Chicken and all them
can grab twelve at a time,
in one hand, too

It's a career,
know what I mean?
Been at it three years myself,
and it's better
than mill work, I'll tell you

Can't believe I can grab
holt a twelve chickens
See here, I grab up three
with my left, pass em to my right
till I got nine there, grab
three more and make for the crate
Fifteen seconds flat

Now, next time you see
one of them chicken trucks
out on U S 601,
You'll right sure know
how them damn chickens
got the hell in there.

The Songwriter Reads About a School Fire

The cries of *Daddy,*
come and get your little
boy as fire closed in
held strong in his mind's
eye till he wrote
the lines about it all—

then he was free. It
wasn't his little one
that passed, but
the forty-eight burned
dead bewitched him
nevertheless.

Such is a kind heart
in times of trial, as
a girl's hand is caught
and pulled into
the loom—another one
gone; a man; a song.

Uwharrie[4]

They say that
once
a man came for boys
here in these hills.

A hunter,
a conscription man.
Come to take them
to fight
Sherman's Georgia fandango.

They hid out
in the rocks, mine pits
of Purgatory,
a hill like
that one
over there.

The boys
wouldn't fight,
but they had spunk.
They shot that man
deader
than a planked shad.

And that man,
the old ones say,
voices low,
that hunter,
that conscription man

still walks up there
on Purgatory,
still walks today.

Wait,
someone says,
Purgatory?
Isn't that over there
where they put
the zoo?

Requiem—Pisgah Covered Bridge

The waters came
and swept it
from its piers
of stone.

Half its shell
washed down;
half folded on
the near bank.

They say it will
rise again, phoenix-
like, in the
green hills.

Will the lovers'
knot from 1920
be there? Or the
planks that

knew cart horses,
mule teams, the
tobacco truck?
They are yesterday

now; the ones who
remember dwindling
slowly, finally,
under the sun.

Dark Mountain

Quartz chill scattered—
miners' tears on
red clay face.

Gopher holes
size of wash tubs—
gold rush spoil.

Eldorado, Ophir—
shuttered windows
like pennied eyes.

Time's days smoothed
tipples, rails,
carts, stamp mills.

Children pan
the Uwharrie,
laughing.

Knowing just this
of the husks and shells
around them.

At a Swimming Pool in the Uwharries

Where do you get a
Confederate flag bikini
these days? Its bottom half-
covers a Desert Storm tattoo
at the base of her spine.

She bobs with the children
and their sea-serpent
float while close-cropped
husband looks on.
The tattoo on his arm

is from shock and awe.
He's still in the Guard;
he's been there, carrying
the weight again, and
now he's going back.

National Forest

Dust-tail gravel road
corkscrews around
Horse Trough Mountain
into dusk. Men took the
trees. New flowers bloom
in the open field.

Day's End, Lake Tillery

Sun dips behind
low mountain,
tinting clean sky.

Brown lake glows
purple-pink, then
dims black.

Rocky cliff plunges
in murk—once free,
clear river.

Below, rusting boil kettle,
unmoved by floods,
last wash-day or
hog killing long past,
shelters a bass.

Hook and leader and
broken line streaming
from its mouth in
silty wash passing,
southward, to the sea.

Along the State Highway to Franklinville

Slow for a textile mill—
brick shell;
hollow egg,
yolk and white blown
through needle holes;

here, bound by mortar,
but the guts
worth anything
auctioned and hauled,
leaving the poison-

laden transformers,
the white clouds
of asbestos and fiber-
glass hanging from
bare steel rafters.

Stop the car to see
Freedom Rock—line
of sight through shattered
mill window, then
collapsed wall

backing the building—
forty-foot, lichened cliff,
framed by rare
Piedmont laurels, shining
in bare winter sun.

Risen

Now the wild rose,
The buckeye, are greening;
The Easter bells ring.

The sun crests God's Acre,
And the last trumpeters
Put down their horns.

A year of promise come—
Or gone. The wrens will
Make a nest.

The dawn wind rushes,
The cedars' roots twine
Those gathered here at last.

When the first bells rang,
We read out, *The Lord
is risen indeed!*

Now we wend homeward
To world and war. The bells
Still, leaving us in need.

"Negroes on the main street of Roxboro, North Carolina"

Gathered on the corner
black men, boys in faded overalls, old coats—
talking price of tobacco, crap
game, new woman in town.

Big-city boy
steps up—
taking photos for FDR.

Might be a cop—
*we ain't done nothing—
anyhow, can't be arguing
with the man.*

They wait while
he sets up—asks
them to stand and talk
just like you were.

Man does his shoot,
and it's a good one,
but there's the sideways
look in their eyes—

tobacco-town street
corner—cold, steel-hard
stare, wishing the picture
man gone.

Regulators

When Fanning kicked the
chair, the man hung
gasping, writhing, shitting.
He and the others
come back, they say,
to gather in the pines
whispering of war and
rumors of war. Last
time was when
fighters boomed over
the bell tower
practicing a run for
Saturday's game.

Crow Hill

The Catholic church, More's
namesake, that crowned
this peak is gone.

Not twentieth century
death of piety—but a parish,
blessed and fruitful,
that outgrew its steeplehouse.

At the hill's foot,
the apartments where men,
flush with GI benefits,
brought young wives
and book bags, will go.

Buses roar upgrade; bikers,
pumping morning rush, reach
for these heights.

Crows that scavenged
the church lot, seeking student
revelers' weekend leavings,
have moved to university parking.

One tops a pole, quawks
for dawn's lift of cold.

Farmhouse, White Oak Church Road, Daybreak

The old gent stands
in the farm's kitchen
garden, stooped, wizened;
tractor cap, woods
jacket and khakis
covering his slumped
frame. Morning sun
cuts sullen, ozone-
laden haze as my
car plunges around
the curve. Slow,
look back—
focus snaps, the
man a scarecrow,
and he, it dwindles
and dims as I
drive away.

Near Hester, N. C.

Twenty years back,
light rails carrying
branch-line freight
bordered a tobacco field

ribboned in spring
with a line of men,
women, children out of
school, to plant, weed, sucker.

The thin, gleaming rails
are gone, their
trace plowed under,
field turned to cotton

the farmer harvests with
machines and a few hands.
The shack by the road
rots, the people gone.

The store where they bought
cokes, where brakies stopped
for vienna-sausage lunch,
careens in still-life, roof beam

broken. The TV antenna,
tied to cement-block stove
chimney, grates and
twists under dull March sun.

Most tobacco warehouses have the cafe open all day and night under the warehouse. Durham, North Carolina[5]

Tobacco Town/Tobacco County (Durham, N.C.)

IN THE SUN AFTER A NOON RAIN, WOODROW STREET

The gutter makes a strange beauty.
Rough granite, concrete,
oil-ribboned water
gurgling under the arch
of a bulged willow-oak root.

Boulevard Sunrise

This deep, green-tunneled place
where the spirit of morning
goes down to dark
like a ripe apple fallen
but not tasted

is quiet in the first hours
as a newspaper vendor
in red vest calls for you
and you do not answer
with two quarters,

is foggy with first light
as sun rises
behind looming trees—
a dull tangerine
in damp, thick sky.

It is good to wake early enough
from time to time
to see this slow dawn.

Durham Street Incident

This was the corner,
Fourth and Club.
The GI wouldn't move
to the back; the driver,
fearing a colored allowed
to bear arms, rose from his
leather-steel bus seat,
pulled a .38 from his pocket
and shot the man
down. The soldier fell,
his drab wool coat
reddening, his uniform cap
rolling into the gutter.

The shot's crack brought
men, women, children
out of shotguns, duplexes
to stare. *Another good man
done gone.*

They renamed it; Fourth
is Berkeley Street now.

Revisiting Liberty Warehouse

There's a padlock on the door
at the Liberty Cafe. I peer
through the window
under a forever-dark neon sign—

the counter's gone, the sink
pipes capped. I remember
the call—*Country
sausage, links or red hots?*—

when I ate breakfast here while
Goodyear worked on my
car. Clatter of dishes, tang
of frying liver mush.

I pull away from the window,
walk past the drive-on-in
door where men chanted
Sold L&M, sold American.

Looking for Blind Boy Fuller's Grave[6]

Children play, cars drive
by on the four-lane,
joggers and bikers
pass on the Tobacco trail.

There's one marker left,
part of the cemetery's
paved over in front
of the daycare.

He lies here—*hey, Blind Boy,
step it up and go*—put
a dime in the jar—
play those blues, boy—

for the farmers with
bankrolls, the long
green, last cash money
till next year's auction.

Blind Boy is gone,
the warehouses torn
down, cigarette machines
stilled. The factories

are condos; God's acre
is a parking lot.

North Durham Homeplace

Tobacco barns lean—
old man stands
corn-stalk straight
beside.

His fields lost to new-
growth loblollies,
furrows covered
with fallen needles.

Wild blackberries
ramble over rusted
fence by green-
scummed farm pond.

Muskrat plashes
as the visitor
stalks stapling-choked
road to his car,

slams the door. Engine
roars, tires grind,
auto's passage fades
to a bobwhite's call.

The View from the Porch

The semi-divided four-lane
thrusts straight through
an old millpond—mill
and dam to the left
viewed northbound.

Pipe culverts under the road
link the waters.

Canada geese, a few
domestic fowl, cluster
by the pond shore—they're
used to the rush
of cars.

Someone lives in the mill—
lawn chairs, bicycle,
rusty grill repose on
a slab by the front door.

Once men sat by the stove
inside, or out here by
the vanished pumps, sipped
bad coffee, white lightning
as their grain was ground.

Today, an occasional
eighteen-wheeler, ambulance,
fire truck livens the view
of mobile, metal boxes
and asphalt—concrete slab.

New Legend of the Flat River

What survival
strides these rocks

above thread-
dwindled Flat?

Poison ivy chokes
the path, water

creeps tan. Dwarf
blackberry, fox

grape, cat brier
green forest floor.

Brilliant in day,
fog-clad in star-

capped, gust-
wind, devil-dark

night. The man at
Tirzah store says

don't walk there
come dark, they'll

be sodding one
new-made grave.

Roadside Memorial

Plastic guitar, fireman's hat
nailed to a tree
at the side of a county
road. Pull off—

read name, date: *September 6,
1996*. Eleven years gone.

Wonder if passersby
see this icon; whether they guess

at men in black coats,
fire helmets, gathered
around a crushed truck—

at EMT's covering
this watcher in the night,

volunteer called away early
by static-laden radio message:

*Ten-four, Bahama fire
dispatch, I'm on my way.*

Orange Factory Revisited[7]

The road plunges into a new
lake—where looms once wove
broadcloth. Foundation
lines can be seen when
water is clear,

resurface in periodic
droughts. Church on the hill,
last survivor, steeple calling
to the sky, looms
above gray waters.

Fisherman in a jon boat
trolls. Line snags
on a stump—once a shade tree.
He stops, cusses, spits, cuts
filament, re-rigs, moves on.

The Caller Visits the Section Boss

It was a hell-hot day
when that decapod
derailed. Old Wash
kept the boys in time.

The sixty-pound was bent
like Gert's hair ribbon.
Took two days to
line that track.

Old Wash says, *Member that
one up by Hester? Bet that
wheel set's still lyin
there, even with the iron
took up.*

Gert brings tea,
sets glasses on
the carport wall.

Got a piece of that iron,
I say, *here in the cubby.*
Old Wash gets up, limps
over, has a gander.

Sure does look thin now, boss,
he says.

Gert stands in the
door. I know she don't
want no coloreds in
her house.

Lyndover Farm

The tobacco field's tight
green rows faded
spiked brown.

Sunrise pushes
orange light through
the loblollies.

No whistle sounds;
the morning train
taken off long ago.

The log barn
slumps, clay washing
out of its chinks.

The bride is
awake and making
coffee. She watches

a red fox pad
the stubble for
bobwhite. Its crimson

coat, bushed tail, the
smell of fresh coffee,
fixes the moment.

She thinks, *I will
remember this.*

And does, even when
her new man
is gone.

Along the Old Durham Branch

Last train cannon-
balled down the line,

rails rust in
weeds and briar.

Tractor's throaty cough,
and charge through fields

to home: side door swings,
shuts out darkness.

Waving furrows,
snaking like those tracks,

turn the upper-
forty corner.

No suckers or bright-leaf
flowers in this plot.

Another falling sun
closes the west.

The Slave Barn

There's a wasp's nest
in the rafters, square-
hewn timbers raised
about eighteen-sixty. In
the grove, four grey
cabins, cedars
in the yards.

Cars rush by on Old
Oxford. No whistle or
bell strikes the air—
train's twenty
years gone. Horton
Grove is still and,
where mud-room post,
floor joist, touches
clay, cabins, barn are
returning earthward.

But, now and again,
crush of gravel on
tires, door slam, light
footfalls, a step, creak
on the porch.

At Stagville Plantation

The barn is a ship
turned turtle to the sun,
pegged ribs clad
with tin and clapboard—
built by hands who
knew the sea.

Turned, to ply the waves
from Africa, it would be
a sturdy craft, carrying
the eggshells of men's lives
to leaf, boll-filled fields
in a far land.

To the Eno[8]

Roar-riven valley
crouches in dreams
like a sphinx.
They were to
fill this, it
too could vanish.
That power and
the good not the
same, it seems.
The river pours
on, tangy with mud,
iced with froth.
Beauty and everyday
be one in our sight.

The path dips—

face-to-face with
frost-white curlicues
gleaming in new-
risen sun—

husks of last
year's weeds
at the power-line
right-of-way.

Winter Heron

Tall, gaunt, blue-gray
shadow.

Fishing the river
alone.

Here out of its
season.

Where does it roost till
nesting time comes?

Heron Flight

Soundless shadow
in still water, long
wings silent, slips

away. Forest
hushed, cars rush
on distant highway,

crow quawks—
great bird rises
above tree line
towards new day.

Flood Following Drought

Live again,
the river sings
through rocks.

Silt and swept
grass bank-side tell
stories of the rain.

The underground
stream, forced topside,
wanes and returns

earthward. What
once was cannot
be, what was

given is used
up. Hurricanes will
sweep, waters flood

again. Don't paste
the leaves to the trees:
they must fall.

Two March Sundays

Last week, bare ground
speckled with sprigs
of Christmas-tree fern.

This week, dense in
trout lily, May apple
like sky salted with stars.

Hurricane Wood

Tornadoes snap
trees off even.
Hurricanes blow
them smartly down.

All pointing leeward:
ground battle-pocked
with root holes
like old photos
of the Somme.

Imagine standing here—
trees corkscrewing,
bending, leaning;
freight-train noise
all around.

Some say nature's
always lovely
but this does raise
certain doubts.

A Place in All Seasons

There is something to be said
for seeing a place in all seasons.
April's minute, glimmering flowers,
September's boiling, ruddy waters,
January's skeletal branches.

The old road, dipping to the river,
once rutted by buckboards
carting corn to the mill.
Now dented by walkers' shoes
and the hooves of morning deer.

There is something to be said
for seeing a place in all seasons.
Last summer's insistent cicadas
missing this July but
coming back in sixteen years.

The great blue heron,
appearing unexpected,
gliding silently downriver.
Seeking its secret,
August roost.

There is something to be said
for seeing a place in all seasons.
For taking the path, rain or sun,
one step, one leaf,
one root at a time.

The Slide

Along the Eno, beavers
don't build lodges—they
burrow into the bank.
Fran's waters took them.

Last fall, a slide
appeared in clay
at waters' edge. A
beaver or otter—

couldn't find
beaver sign on the
trees; the tracks weren't
clear in Piedmont

mire. Finally,
at least,
something
was back.

Two weeks ago, a
storm—now, leaves
fill the slide, no
tracks, the game path

into the woods grows
faint, lost, as spring
fills canopy, understory, and
birds trill in the trees.

Eno Bank

The laurels stand green, rare,
almost out-of-place.

Bloom each June, hug the same
north-slope land.

Changed plans halted road work,
saved the still, small cove.

A tiny victory for what was, is,
over what, mostly, shall be.

At the Little River Trail

The path winds and dips—
I take it, my boots scattering
scree and lumps
of clay. At the bottom,

the river, strong spring flow
past rocks and fallen
trees. Then, a plashing—
two fish spawning

in the current.
Beyond, downed sycamore
crosses and a quick
shape with legs,

a long tail hears my tread,
dives to safety.
Mink, otter,
tremendous salamander?

I trample this trail,
but little I know,
so little I know, of what
lies beside and around it.

Little River Bridge

Rust-red rails, weed-grown,
converge at a point lost in scrub,

run flat, straight, and true
under black-iron arch of a truss

massed over narrow river
joined to the Eno, then the Flat,

makes the Neuse. The Neuse
flows to the sea. We dammed it.

Makes a lake, starts right here,
muddy field of deadened water.

Little, Eno, Flat. Neuse. We
dammed it. We dammed them.

BUYOUT

No photo for those years.
Daddy—Mr. Til Mangum—
sold more than
his allotment. That's
all—sold more than
his allotment. For two
years, we'd visit
him when we could—
see him through smeared
glass, talk on a sputtering
phone. Seems so strange
now—it's gone, all gone:
Daddy, the allotment,
the tractor, the farm.

I close the album, Judy
starts the dishwasher,
slosh whine and
clatter doubles up with
the kids watching TV
to comfort me, to bring
it on home.

*Fish sign,
Washington, North Carolina*[9]

Coast

Warren Plains Depot[10]

Smoke-belching supply
to Lee in Richmond.
Grey-clad men on platform,
one with a pinned-up
pants leg. The town
didn't want progress, put
its main-line station here
in the cotton fields.

Now, tourists mount the steps,
hunt for cheap antiques.
The main line is a rutted
weed-track edging the pastures.
Night-gaunt, unpainted,
its first army overtaken
by these strangers, this
dream-house soldiers on.

Bentonville Battlefield

From this house
where legs, arms,
piled to the sill,
they come.

Spooking deer,
frightening hunters,
chilling the dawn-
walking farmer.

What keeps them here,
beyond forgetting,
we do not know.

A grind, a groan, a
shattered arm drops,
the end of surgery
but not of pain.

Later, gone to
dust, the end of
life but not of
phantoms.

New Bypass

The four-lane cuts fields laden with
cotton bales—white blocks
the size of trucks, bundles of cash. But
it bypasses town. The 1844 church
is a museum that didn't take,
its old cemetery buried under a two-
star day care's parking lot. Jobs
at the nut-snack-fruit factory
are the best game in town. Even
the Hardee's, once thronged
by beachgoers emptying bladders,
is closed.

On the bypass, cars rush
from city to shore, windows up, air
conditioners blasting. With panes down,
whiff the swamp-rot—
like wet leaves decaying
in November—and hear the *whup,
whup, whup* of guard-rail
posts, keeping cars
out of the canal when drivers drowse
off, sand-bound, on this slab
of somewhere to somewhere
through nowhere.

Three Portraits

The curve in the road
is gentle, like swells
on the sea.

The town is tired,
too large since water-
wheels stilled, looms
stopped weaving, yarn
mills ceased to spin.

At roadside, shed wall
with three portraits of Jesus—
at the left, wearing a cloak,
walking the paths;
on the right, by God's side.

And, in the center,
waist-view, naked,
hands raised waiting
for the spikes.

A flash by, the scene
is gone—then
rivers, pocosins,
the journey home.

First Growth Cypress, Williamston, North Carolina

Dark waters' dead calm
pegged by sharp knees
circling gaunt survivor,
ancient one.

Think back the years
to the quick flash that
topped it, crippled it,
saved it from the saw.

When the Fish Come Back

The state won't let us
dip our nets
in the Roanoke
this spring.

The fish we'll grill, salt
hail from Canada.

When the herring come back,
maybe next year,
we'll get a keg, have
a good fry.

I don't remember days
before motorboats, mills,
dams, rules from Raleigh—
when the river ran silver

with fish. It's all water
under the bridge now.

When the herring come back,
though, maybe next year,
we'll get some liquor, have
a good fry.

Frost Morning

Nut-brown ditch framed
by snow-cropped towpath
runs straight as plumb-bob string
to heart of the great swamp.

The man walks uncertain
in dim-moon dark.
Owl hunt, deer stand,
wildcat pace, unseen.

No place to end. Come dawn
he turns back—from holes
worn in snow by
pawing, cloven hooves.

At the Old Town Cemetery, Beaufort

On these lichened stones pours down
haze-refracted sun.
Below, the frozen men moulder.

Blocks away, a post-office
mural shows the story. Gray
mariners carried, stiff, to shore.

People at the stamp
window, pocketing change,
don't look up. They're
used to the scene.

Boxed Longleafs

In this part of the wood,
each great pine bears a scar
from the base up past
your eyes.

Rectangular, incised into
heartwood, serrated with
sharp lines. Clean and new
and polished.

Unhealing marks of
a man born before
last century's turn.

Conjure in the Southport Burying Ground[11]

Graves of infants, children
marked with cowries,
bits of red ribbon.

Can we capture a soul
for service if called
before its time?

The root doctor chants
at midnight, the moon
waxes, just past new.

Cut bad by her man,
a woman slips away,
hoping the child-spirit

will protect her,
release her from this
careless love.

Summer Dawn, Kitty Hawk

Walking the dull, heartsick beach,
not believing it's June.
Passing a grandmother, mother, kid
haltingly looking for shells.

Ahead a strange lump
glowing the salt mist.
At first, chilled, seeing a body.
Then, gaudy bloated sofa cushion.

And then—new-dead sea turtle
laced with bright lines:
writing in pink paint.
Might say, "sick." Could be, "kill."

Death painted a puzzle
I'm thinking I can't solve.
I'm wishing I could stop the kid.
Slowly, she stumbles closer.

Swan Quarter Landing

A January wind
whips the ferry.
Twelve knots and
the boat adds five or ten.

Cold air cutting
through the warp
and weft
of my coat;
through my jeans,
shirt and undershirt.

The lounge is warm;
there are Lance and
Pepsi machines.
Just before landing
the ferry men
unchock the cars,
then stand at the bow.

A life
this different from mine
couldn't be imagined.

NOTES

The title of this book, Old North, *is a short version of a period nickname for North Carolina, the "Old North State." This nickname is reflected in many things about North Carolina, including the state song, "The Old North State," and the state toast, the best-known (first) stanza of which goes:*
Here's to the land of the long leaf pine,
The summer land where the sun doth shine,
Where the weak grow strong and the strong grow great,
Here's to "Down Home," the Old North State!

1. *Fiddlin' Bill Hensley, mountain fiddler, Asheville, North Carolina. Photo by Ben Shahn, 1937.* Library of Congress, Prints & Photographs Division, *FSA-OWI Collection, LC-USF33-006258-M3.*

2. *On the night she [Laura Foster] was to meet [Tom] Dula, she left her home, never to be seen alive again. While it is not known for certain what happened that evening, many of the stories that have grown out of the folklore of the time implicate Ann Melton in some way.... on Dula's word, Melton was acquitted of the crime.*

3. *Negroes on the main street of Roxboro, North Carolina. Jack Delano, May 1940.* Library of Congress, Prints & Photographs Division, *FSA-OWI Collection, LC-USF33-020508-M5.*

4. *The Uwharrie region, the setting for this and the following five poems, is a range of old mountains located in the North Carolina Piedmont, at about the geographic center of the state. The Uwharries are roughly south of Greensboro, north of the South Carolina border, east of Charlotte and west of U.S. 220. They are small, gentle mountains topping out at under 1,000 feet in elevation. The Uwharrie region is famous for its folklore, especially for its supernatural legends.*

5.   Most tobacco warehouses have the cafe open all day and night under the warehouse. Durham, North Carolina. Marion Post Wolcott, believed to have been taken in November, 1939. Library of Congress, Prints & Photographs Division, FSA-OWI Collection, LC-USF33-030676-M3.

6.   Fulton Allen, aka "Blind Boy Fuller," Piedmont blues musician, b. Wadesboro, N.C., 1907, d. Durham, N.C., 1941

7.   Continue along Orange Factory Rd. across the Little River Reservoir, a Durham [N.C.] water supply. Its construction in the 1980s flooded the village of Orange Factory. Built in 1852 by John H. Webb and John C. Douglas, the water-powered textile factory was called Orange Factory because it was the first factory in what was then Orange County. Around it stood a village of the same name with houses for workers, a store, a school, church, and other mill buildings. — "Driving Tour of the Little River"

8.   This poem, and the nine following poems, is set in Eno River State Park, especially the Pump Station Trail section of the park in northwestern Durham County.

9.   Fish sign, Washington, North Carolina. John Vachon, April 1938. Library of Congress, Prints & Photographs Division, FSA-OWI Collection, LC-USF33-001110-M3.

10.   Constructed 1864.

11.   To understand the wide range of materials used in conjure bags, and the various local names applied to them... one should read the two long and detailed chapters, 'Voodooism' and 'Conjuration' in Puckett... Puckett contains an excellent treatise on the various other uses to which graveyard dirt is put... also the use of graveyard dirt in a conjure bag... and the planting of graveyard dirt to counteract a conjuration.
—The Frank C. Brown Collection of North Carolina Folklore

www.ingramcontent.com/pod-product-compliance
Lightning Source LLC
LaVergne TN
LVHW091314080426
835510LV00007B/496